GUIDANCE FOR INDEPENDENT SENIORS

COMMON SENSE GUIDE FOR WELLNESS AND DAILY LIFE MANAGEMENT

William M. Teringo

DEDICATION

This book is dedicated to Starr, my wife of forty-five years who has stood with me through the trials and tribulations of the past. In all my endeavors, Starr has encouraged and supported each, as she has with the writing of this book.

Starr is the stalwart of our independent retirement years making each day loving and pleasant with a constant vigilance of our health maintenance requirements. She gives the reasons to look forward to all the years we will be spending together.

TABLE OF CONTENTS

FORWARD

I am not a physician, but I am an independent senior citizen and recipient of the new medical practice procedures. The following information is a commonsense guide in laymen's terms to the extent one must be aware of and self-manage personal health care.

An independent senior citizen is an individual that is self-sufficient who lives alone or with a spouse, companion or relative and is not dependent for care of an assisted living facility or a nursing home.

Establish a relationship with a primary care physician for regular wellness appointments to constantly monitor health issues. Waiting too long to see a physician when feeling ill can allow an illness to develop into a dangerous stage. What was in younger years a minor illness or an inconvenience changes as one ages. As a senior all illnesses need to be attended to promptly by a primary care physician before it becomes a major health event leading to serious complications which can adversely affect current and future medical issues.

A referral to a specialist for additional physical evaluation and scans can be a positive step in the patient's wellbeing if truly necessary to solve a complex medical issue. A generalized exploratory referral for testing or a procedure without a clear initial medical purpose or objective other than a let's look and see may be unnecessary. By becoming part of the exploratory medical assembly line medicine can even be counterproductive, costly and time consuming.

The topics put forth discuss the commonsense measures that are needed to aid the patient in the control of personal wellbeing, changing medical needs, understanding when confronted for the first time with necessary preparation and what to expect during the processing for a procedure. The topics cover a wide range of health issues and circumstances. Certain topics may not initially be applicable to all but are available for future reference as needed. Included throughout the topics is how to communicate and establish a patient to physician relationship that will ultimately be beneficial to the success of long-term health.

THE MEDICAL ASSEMBLY LINE

What is the Medical Assembly Line? To explain a simple example goes like this. The big toe has been stubbed, it is swollen, really hurts and it is difficult to walk without pain. An appointment is made with the primary care physician to evaluate the issue. The physician examines the swollen digit and indicates it doesn't seem broken and recommends an off the shelf pain reliever and a referral to a podiatrist (foot doctor) with whom a future appointment is made. The podiatrist agrees that the toe is not broken but to be sure an x-ray will be needed. An appointment is made with the x-ray facility. After the x-ray a return visit to the podiatrist is made to review the results of the x-ray and determine a course of action. At the appointment the diagnosis is that it is not broken, and everything is fine. Guess what the swelling and pain went away weeks ago.

Moral of the story is four medical appointments were made, filling out of numerous repetitive forms and travel to four locations over several weeks for a stubbed toe. Four co-pays where made with the bulk of cost paid by the insurance company and/or Medicare. This is how the Medical Assembly Line works for a very simple non serious event that in the past would be diagnosed and dealt with on the initial medical visit.

For minor medical events it should be considered with the physician's consent to postpone additional medical assembly line visits to allow for normal healing unless there is a compelling reason in the patients' medical history to warrant a further examination.

For major medical events all referrals for additional testing, scans, x-rays, procedures and a visit to a specialist that are ordered by the primary care physician for further evaluation of the possibility of a serious health issue are necessary to properly diagnose and determine the onset or current stage of a serious illness should be complied with. Evaluating a serious illness or possibility of is not the Medical Assembly Line.

Medical test and treatments in today's world are far more advanced than even a decade ago. The primary care physician may be suspicious of an initial diagnosis or progression of a serious medical issue and will want conformation and patient access to specialized treatment. With targeted treatments by specialist who have at their disposal the latest medicines, medical testing and procedural apparatus for life saving and pain relief the benefits of a consultation with a specialist is paramount for specific medical events. It is inevitable that it will be in the patient's best interest to see a specialist for obvious medical events either emergency or exploratory. Exploratory evaluations should be discussed in consultation with the primary care physician and specialist to include reason, necessity, timing and expectation for the additional testing and/or intrusive surgery. Some if not most are blood tests or noninvasive procedures but if surgery is recommended then a second opinion from a like medical practice should be sought.

A patient should not blindly except, ignore or refuse additional procedures without full disclosure and a compelling reason why, other than a simple blood tests, the procedures are necessary and should compare the objectives of both the initiating physician and implementing physician/facility as to the reason for, knowledge of what the procedure involves, dangers and recovery time as in the case of surgery and if negative results what are the next steps to wellness.

After any procedure a consolation with the initiating physician to include reported results generated by the test should be fully evaluated. The evaluation will include the patient's medical history which will also be used in the determination of a course of action if necessary.

PREVENTIVE MEDICINE BASE LINE MARKERS

The need to establish with the primary care physician a dated base line for current and future medical evaluation with ranges of acceptability and established goals. Serious medical issues should be highlighted and addressed separately with an individual base line marker and acceptable wellness improvement target with formal documentation. To establish a base line marker program the initial step is a full comprehensive physical and full range blood work up. This will include a blood work up report submitted by the laboratory that can be used to establish markers based on accepted medical norms. The written report submitted from the blood testing laboratory, results from the physical examination and the reports from specialized test and body scans ordered for an ailment are to be part of establishment of a base line marker program. Questionable results from a blood test may require additional specialized test to establish a marker. The medical status information gathered and used to establish the physical being of the patient using the visual markers will allow the primary care physician during future visits to review updated test results either positive or negative to evaluate overall wellness. Comparison of past and current base line markers will allow the primary care physician to make informed decisions as to current status that the pre-established wellness program is working or requires change, revisions to base line markers and be an alert of possible future problems that can be addressed prior to serious onset. Request copies of data from primary care physician for one's own personal base line marker records.

Prepare written reference questions in advance of a visit to include self-diagnosis comments and stay focused taking the necessary time with the physician until you are satisfied with the explanations. Do not be afraid to ask questions or request explanations of medical terminology. The base line marker documentation and latest available updates should be carried to each visit to a physician with any new updated test and changed information added to the personal base line marker documents.

Establish a protocol with the primary care physician and/or nursing staff to evaluate any new prescriptions issued by other physicians so that they do no counteract current medications. Any issuing physician should be made aware of all medications and treatments currently being taken. See Topic Listing and Control of Medications.

A medical appointment is one of many that the physician will have that day and, in many cases, the only preparation is the glance at the chart during the greeting. Be precise with reason/s for the appointment and understand in detail the prognoses and steps to correct the event to include proper dosages of any medications and their side effects. Discuss other medical topics on the list. Remember when the doctor is finished it is onto the next patient.

The patient should request to be made aware by the primary care physician or executing physician of any additional, no matter how minor, changes to base markers or abnormalities detected in a body scan of any type. Especially if related to a family history generic profile and documented in the patients record for future testing and evaluation.

At any evaluation procedure that a CD or MRI of the results is available acquire a copy for future reference, non-receipt by initiating physician and for a second opinion physician to view.

Be pro-active with preventive vaccine inoculations that are readily available in most case free of or minimum charge at a pharmacy, clinic or physician's office that should be taken as needed, yearly. Besides any special vaccines prescribed by a physician the basic inoculations are Influenza (flu), Pneumonia, Shingles and Tetanus.

LISTING AND CONTROL OF MEDICATIONS

There is a free medication app on most cell phones on which medications can be listed and some with an alert for time of intake. If a cell phone does not come with a medication app there are various apps that can be obtained. Make sure the app can protect entered personal medical information. The cell phone app is fine for listing minimal medication intake and medical issue as a quick personal reference.

For those with more than a few different and complex medical and medication issues, a detailed listing of medications, vitamins, over the counter drugs and their usage should be created. A currently dated and paper written private medication control schedule for usage intake is needed to include personal history that can easily be presented to pertinent medical personal when applicable for review by an attending physician or during a medical event.

The objective of listing and controlling medication intake is to prevent missed dosages and overdosing. Make up two paper printed dated lists of medications being taken. The first list is for control of the scheduling of daily medication intake in a printed format available as needed for filling of medication pill boxes, travel preparations' and review by the primary care physician. It should have titles i.e. Morning (7 AM); Noon (1 PM); Evening (7 PM) and Bedtime as applicable. It should include amount, name of medication, dosage and what aliment. Medications taken more than once per day are to be listed on the schedule for each intake time. The list to include as needed medications, vitamins, over the counter drugs and supplements.

The following examples to be used as needed based on prescription instructions.

Example of daily medication intake:

Morning (7AM)
1 Each Name of medication 50Mg - Sugar
1 Each Name of medication 5mg – Blood Pressure
1 Each Name of medication 40Mg – Cholesterol
1 Each Vitamin B-6 200Mg
        Etc.
Midday (1PM)
1 Each Name of medication 5mg – Thyroid

Evening (7PM)

1 Each <u>Name of medication</u> 5Mg – Blood Pressure

1 Each <u>Name of medication</u> 50Mg – Sugar

      Etc.

Bedtime – Name of Medication – 10Mg – Sleep

As Needed

At bottom of list: 1 EACH <u>Name of</u> medication 10Mg – For knee pain

Include information on vaccine inoculations, diet programs, over the counter permanent medications and highlighted known medication and food allergies. Separately the primary care physician should also verbally be made aware of alcohol usage and the extent of past and current controlled substance drug abuse. The non-acknowledgment can directly affect prescribed medications effectiveness and create major complication with minor or major surgeries.

The second is a condensed simplified listing of all medications, as needed prescriptions, vitamins and supplements with dosage amounts, number of units per day and what aliments they are for. It should also contain information on any medication and food allergies, diet programs and over the counter permanent medications to include listing of current afflictions i.e. Heart issues, Diabetic, COPD and all other permanent health issues.

It is also necessary to make a verbal statement to attending medical professional during any emergency or procedure of any active alcohol and illicit drug use and other private information that could affect the diagnosis and level of care. The second condensed list can be used as an attachment to the requested medication listing in a repetitive form.

Example of Second Condensed list:

Medications Taken Per Day:
2 Each <u>Name of medication</u> 5Mg – Blood Pressure
1 Each <u>Name of medication</u> 40Mg – Cholesterol
1 Each Vitamin B6 200Mg
      Etc
As Needed
As needed 1 EACH Name of medication 10Mg for knee pain

At bottom of list:
Aliments: Type 2 Diabetic – High Blood Pressure etc.
Inoculations: Flu, Pneumonia etc.

Primary care Physician – Dr. <u>Name doctor</u> –
Emergency phone number of doctor

The second condensed list should be available for medical emergency situations and carried on one's person to supply vital information to emergency care givers at point of event and to emergency room personnel.

Both lists should always be regularly updated with any new, deleted and changes to dosages of medications as they occur. A yearly evaluation of the lists by the primary care physician on what medications are no longer needed or are to be changed to newer more effect drugs should be conducted and documented.

A specific established daily time for medication intake as specified on the medication list needs to be followed exactly so that any missed medication intake is easily apparent and can be adjusted for with no likelihood of overdosing.

When away from home during medication intake time/s carry a small pill box with adequate medications to maintain proper intake scheduling.

REPETITIVE FORMS

Unfortunately, there is not a standard format used by medical offices or facilities that can be filled out once, copied and submitted. The forms are designed to acquire general medical background needed by the treating physician or for a specialized diagnosis or procedure.

To assist in simplifying the repetitive form filling out at an initial or the yearly up dating request by a physician or medical treatment procedure facility. Take advantage of areas of standardization on all forms. A list of medications as outlined in topic Listing and Control of Medication – Second Condensed List can be pre-printed and used as an attachment to physical paperwork or aid in entering online registration forms. Full disclosures of information on the forms is essential and question check offs accurate. There are no maybes when evaluating and checking off an answer, either it is a medical issue or is not. Preprinted medication list and general well fair information will reduce the entry burden. To avoid searching for insurance or Medicare identification numbers or proper spelling of a medication or affliction just list them on the medication list for easy reference.

The form package also includes a series of required to sign legal liability waivers that are unavoidable.

MEDICATIONS - ONE SIZE DOES NOT FIT ALL

Many medications have multiple usages, ranges of dosages and contain different chemical formulations with some creating a more costly prescription than may be needed. When a medicine is prescribed in almost all cases the physician is unaware of the cost and is basing the decision on what has been prescribed in the past for other patients with similar ailments or is currently being promoted by the pharmaceutical companies for a particular ailment though it may also be suitable for other ailments. The patient is relying on the doctor's decision to have the best interest of the patient which is the case.

When a medication is prescribed ask if all the chemical compounds that make up the formulations are necessary for medicating a particular ailment to include recommended manufacturer dosage amount. If not, what other medications are targeted specifically for the diagnosis to include a less expensive generic. The physician or nurse can easily research possible alternatives in the available office medical data base along with side effects and adverse reaction involving current medications. Take the recommended prescription to a pharmacy along with any named alternatives supplied by the medical office to determine the least costly. Ask the pharmacy what the cost or co-pay of the named alternative medications will be based on Medicare and private insurance. Stay with the prescription if only a nominal difference in cost between various like medications. If there is a substantial cost savings for the same curative factors, then contact the physician's office for an evaluation and changed prescription.

An online search can also be done by the patient by entering – Name of prescribed medication and the word generic. Also, side effects of individual medications can be reviewed.

It may take several attempts by the attending physician to adjust the type of medication and dosage amounts to find the proper balance for the patient's treatment. This may require additional testing to determine effectiveness based on established base line markers. Evaluation by the primary care physician needs to be immediately addressed if the affliction worsens or at a minimum at time of yearly physical.

This is what is known as taking aggressive personal health care action to assure wellbeing and to assist the primary care physician to find medications and dosage amounts that are suitable and less expensive to long term wellness needs.

MANAGING SIDE EFFECTS & ALLERGIC REACTIONS

Side effects of medications can possibly be more harmful than the affliction. To avoid an initial episode of adverse side effects or allergic reactions discuss newly prescribed medication and the possibility of reaction in combination with current medications and known personal history with the prescribing physician. Be suspicious of a new medication formulation that contains a known drug that in the past has possibly caused an adverse reaction. Compare a possible or real side effect occurrence to the immediate wellness benefits of a prescribed medication to determine further usage. A side effect may be readily noticeable i.e. diarrhea, nausea or vomiting, dizziness, rash and muscle pain etc. But may initially be undetected and effecting internal organs upon initial usage or over a long term i.e. liver, heart rhythm, pancreas etc. therefore periodic testing needs to be done if there is suspicion or physical evidence of a long-term negative reaction to the medications listed side effects. If a major side effect problem surfaces alternative medications need to be fully investigated for their wellness effectiveness and the reduction of side effects. In addition, side effects may be generated from the regular usage of over the counter drugs.

With all new prescribed medications that can cause major personal side effects the user should prepare a written list, with an area for comments to include number and severity of episodes of the side effects listed on the provided medical guide information sheet supplied with the medication or any unusual physical or mental events that may be associated with the medication after taking to include allergic reactions. Investigate the side effects and possibility of increased reaction to current allergies online by entering the name and dosage with the words side effects. Use the prepared list to monitor physical reactions over the first few weeks noting none, un-comfortableness, moderate or severe to each side effect. Add any reactions to the medication that may not be listed. If severe, moderate or uncomfortable symptoms emerge do not ignore the warning signs contact the prescribing physician immediately.

A decision concerning severe side effects to the patient should be based on the prescribed medication's side effects to include the use of another medication option and possibility of reduced side effects to achieve the same wellness goal. If no other medication is available to eliminate the physical side effect/s or allergic issues, then there are four possible options. Acceptance of the side effect, use of an additional medication to relieve the side effect, dietary regiment where applicable and forgoing the medication because the side effect is more harmful than the affliction. The options must be an informed and thought out decision by both patient and primary care physician based on current and long-term treatment options. The patient must determine the degree of un-comfortableness that is acceptable in relationship to the benefits of the medication.

The pharmaceutical companies list all possibilities of a negative reaction to a medication discovered in clinical trials. The percentage of provability is not listed. Reaction to the drug will depend on the individual patient's physical being, allergic reaction and other medications being ingested that in combination can trigger a side effect. There is no formula to detect if a patient will experience a severe, moderate or passive side effect and only the use of the medication will determine usable status.

MANAGEMENT OF INDIVIDUAL HEALTH CARE

SELF EVALUATION

It is important not to ignore the body's signs of change in physical, mental and simply put the gut feelings of wellness. Each person should be self-aware and if not take the time to evaluate status of current medical conditions along with known genetic family history to establish a personal thought out base line of the body's current medical status.

Self-diagnostic steps to detect the possible onset of undiagnosed or escalation of current health issues should be done on a regular schedule. Detection is a major part of early identification of a future, increase of or reoccurrence of a health risk. Simple personal observations can be mind settling or bring an awareness of changes that need further investigation. Acute or perceived minor physical changes should be noted and discussed with the primary care physician or administering specialist to determine the validity of the self-diagnoses.

The pre-establishment of a personal standard of normalcy of the body and body functions will aid in the detection of acute changes. Short term body irregularities to include aches and pains that are a reaction to outside of the body influences or a part of daily activity unless persistent need not be immediately judged as acute. No one is more aware of body changes and better suited than the person doing the self-evaluation to realize both acute and normal age-related changes.

There are so many variables when performing a self-evaluation and a single finding can represent a host of possible health risks. Do not overreact to a finding. Not all evidence of abnormalities is life threatening. A finding of a minor painful or an embarrassing condition may not affect overall health. That is not to say they should not be brought to the attention of the primary care physician during a scheduled visit. If self-examination has uncovered the possibility of a future perceived life-threatening abnormality a further detailed final determination as to the possible cause can only be done with a physician's physical examination to include blood, urine and minimal specialized testing as applicable to determine actuality. If initial testing indicates the presents of an acute problem then the immediate full resources of all medical specialties needed to determine severity, course of action and medical procedures should be utilized to achieve wellbeing.

Procedures for self-examination are visual, touch and feel, flexing of body areas and a thought review of abnormal current physical and mental events to determine wellness status. Listen to what the body is telling of possible changes. The self-examination is done to reveal both the positive or negative results to the pre-established physical and mental base line markers as outlined in the topic Preventive Medicine. A record of findings should be dated and documented each time the self-evaluation is performed for follow up awareness and future consultation with the primary care physician.

Visual examination of the body during bath time should look for rashes, abscesses, crusty skin, skin sores and discoloration (Melanoma), cysts, toe nail fungus, blood in body waste, enlargement of moles with ragged edges, loose teeth or bleeding gums and any out of the norm skin and body unnatural appearing disorders i.e. bumps, knots, bulging areas and non-healing bruises.

Touch and feel examination can be done in privacy at any time. Signs of medical issues can be reaction by pain to a push into the torso area, back, legs or arms and throat areas. Additional signs are swelling in the groin, pain in legs joints when rising from a seated position, lumps in the breast or other body areas, fluid buildup especially ankles and feet, inability to tightly grip objects, flexing muscle distress, irregular breathing, pressure in the chest when climbing stairs and extended walking, painful urination and any directly associated signs with a pre-diagnosed aliment. Blood pressure self-testing on a regular bases with a inexpensive home unit or kiosk at a pharmacy can if in a negative range be relayed to the primary care physician for evaluation to prevent issues that are treatable with medications such as the possibility of a stroke and other previously undiagnosed ailments.

Feelings that something is not right with general body wellness or a specific area not identified in an external self-examination such as a drastic change to normal schedule of body functions, uneasiness or slight pain in internal torso area when making abrupt movements and any abnormal physical sensations should not be ignored and discussed with the primary care physician.

Chronic Fatigue can be an indication of many health problems that need to be evaluated and tested to determine the exact cause. Chronic fatigue can be a sign of heart disease, thyroid disorder, diabetes, anemia, cancer, chronic infection, autoimmune disorder, sleep disorder (Sleep APNEA), eye strain, HIV, mental disorder, pulmonary disease (COPD), inflammatory bowl, anxiety, over whelming stress and reaction to medications both prescribed and over the counter.

Periodic fatigue is a physical or a mental event and can be a normal reaction to overwork, over exercising or lack of, boredom, moderate stress or anxiety and be alleviated with rest and relaxation. It can also be a normal senior aging process requiring a midday nap to reenergize both the body and mind.

Mental self-diagnosis for management of physical health care purposes is a simple process of serious thought taking into consideration the possible onset of changes in the lack of concentrations, short term memory loss, slurring of words, lasting depression, shying away from activities, being resentful and feeling of inadequacy. Though seemingly some if not all are signs of mental dysfunction it may be a case of improper management of medication as to dosages, side effects or a mixture of counter acting medication creating a reaction negative to one's normal being. Medication groupings should be investigated prior to additional psychological consultation.

Alzheimer's and Dementia self-evaluation of the initial early signs of symptoms are hard to self-analyze. Both afflictions seemingly are the same but there is a slight difference even though many of the symptoms initially are the same with similar final results. Alzheimer's is a slow methodical creeping mental disease whereas dementia is aggressive, and both are associated mostly with aging. Early warning signs to the onset of both afflictions though not exclusive are short term memory, bouts of loss of awareness, inability to make judgments, loss of common sense, misplacing of items, inability to focus, hallucinations, illusions, sentence construction difficulties, wandering, and aggressiveness. The onset of the afflictions may not be fully recognized through self-evaluation. Respectful comments made by others that match symptoms should not be ignored an alert one to recognizing the necessity to seek early treatments that are currently available.

Self-observations of minor mental lapses that are part of the normal senior aging process need to be considered prior to making a judgment that they are signs of a major mental disorder. As most senior citizen age there is a slow normal progression of a reduction of mental capabilities to include very short-term minor memory loss such as item misplacement and why did I come in here as examples.

Accidents causing cuts and bruises and pulled muscles if properly cared for should be self-evaluated for the degree of severity prior to contacting a physician or going to an emergency room. Falling by seniors is more serious and if not in immediate need of emergence care the injury should be evaluated as soon as possible by a physician for additional treatment and medication to prevent infection. The fall in itself may not be critical but can cause other serious events throughout the body.

Known negative genetic family history and severity should be discussed with primary care physician and the patient informed of the signs of possible onset. Yearly physicals should include emphasis on testing for signs of onset of the genetic affliction and become part of the medical record. This will alert the primary care physician to engage in early treatment to avoid future major events. Not all genetic negative history is passed on to every generation so both parental and grandparent genetic information when available should be part of the patient family record.

Present all self-evaluation information to the primary care physician for evaluation when negative results are present that may reflect a wellness problem. Discuss if the changes found through self-examination are signs of a new illness, change to current wellness status, normal aging process or are related to side effects from prescription medications, over the counter drugs, dosage's amount or a possible allergic reaction event.

VITAMIN AND MINERAL SUPPLEMENTS

Vitamins are an essential daily part of a senior citizen wellness program. Over the counter multivitamins offer averaged dosages of daily basic vitamin and mineral requirements for various age groups to include over 65. A general one size fits all vitamins and minerals even when developed for a specific age group cannot take into account individual current and changing nutritional requirements. Over the counter multivitamins may not have sufficient dosages or have the additional special vitamins and minerals supplements as part of their formulation that may be required by an individual's aging body to maintain a nutritional wellness and energy acceptable standard.

As one ages vitamins and minerals need to be adjusted to account for bodily changes. Based on an individual's age, general diet, volume and nutritional value of food intake, number of meals per day, inability to fully process foods, medical issues and exercise a needed balance and increase of specific and essential vitamins and minerals may be required. Increases in calcium, iron, various vitamins B, C, D & E etc. to include supplements like fish oil for the heart to name a few of nutrients that the body may be currently starved of.

Within a full scope blood test during an annual physical or intermediate test can reveal deficiencies, in need of adjustment and introduction of additional vitamins and minerals to balance nutritional wellbeing. Testing should be repeated on a yearly minimum for adjustments to the bodies aging changing requirements.

The primary care physician taking into considerations age, lifestyle, food intake, physical being, medications possibly affected by the intake or overdose of specific vitamins and minerals should evaluate and create a program for the patient with proper dosages to balance nutritional wellness.

NATURAL FOOD NUTRIENTS

The following is not a diet plan but a way to assist a patient to find knowledge of natural foods with the nutrients that are beneficial for a specific affliction and what foods are not recommended. Natural food nutrients added to the diet are to boost but not replace medications, vitamins and minerals prescribed by a physician or dietitian. Natural foods are not a cure.

It would be too long a list to match all afflictions to benefits of natural food nutrients. It is recommended that the patient take advantage of the physician's recommendations or the information available on the internet by specifying an affliction.

Enter: **Nutritional diet food for (the affliction name) disease**. As an example, enter Nutritional diet food for heart disease. The entry will in almost all cases bring immediate search informational results to include wellness tips but could require some additional minor searching for more probing results. The information obtained should always come from accredited medical sources. Beware of false advertising claims from non-accredited vendors. See the Topic: What Seniors Need to Know About Medical Advertisements for additional information.

General practitioners do not normally introduce the use of natural nutrients in their prescribed treatments. It is up to the patient to investigate and establish a suitable natural nutritional intake program with the primary care physician or dietitian oversight that is in accordance with current medical issues.

A natural nutritional program can easily be incorporated into the lifestyle of the patient by using the natural foods recommended for main courses, side dishes, snacks and additive to a recipe. Be aware of the possibility of allergic events and adverse reaction of medications when a new dietary supplement is introduced into the digestive system. If a negative event occurs immediately stop intake of the natural food until consolation with primary care physician. Be attentive as to what, when and how much is being eaten to determine, after testing, the benefits of nutritional value and if it is truly effective for wellness or has no effect on the ailment even over a long period.

If for medical reason a major change in diet and nutritional intake is prescribed to include natural nutrients for a limited or extended time period, it is critical that it is overseen by a primary care physician or a certified dietitian with pre-established goals. The reaction to major dietary changes can adversely affect the body and needs to be monitored and documented for reactions to current medications and general health.

EXERCISE PROGRAMS FOR SENIORS

There are numerous exercises programs designed for seniors of all ages on the internet and will require review to determine which exercise routines will best fit current age, mobility, medical condition, living environment and local seasonal weather changes. Multiple exercise plans adjusted to seasonal changes that curtail outside exercise and travel due to heat, cold or inclement weather that obtain near or same daily end results need to be part of the overall wellness exercise program planning.

Physicians do not normally go into detail on exercise programs other than the need to exercise and the mention of walking unless an exercise is specific to physical therapy wellness after an accident or surgery. It is up to the individual to be pro-active in the creation of a daily exercise program best suited to personal physical abilities and fitness goals.

Type of exercises, repetitions, strength requirements, involvement in sports and walking or running endurance will vary between individuals and age groups. The differences between a normal active 65-year-old and active 80-year-old and the ages between in exercise abilities and stamina are enormous taking into account additional ailments and normal muscle deterioration. Past medical issues, major surgeries, awareness of potential future physical problems, necessity of rest periods and other ailments i.e. COPD must be a part of the equation when assembling a personal exercise program. Avoid exercises with body positions, movements and lift requirements that could aggravate current and anticipated future medical events. Research and select the best long term individual indoor and outdoor exercises from internet programs containing different exercises within the stamina range and goals suitable for current age, physical limits and medical status.

Programs for individuals with a physical status or handicap that cannot support strenuous and mobile exercise i.e. wheelchair and bed bound there are internet sites offering a variety of specially designed exercises. Professional assistance is also available through local governmental and private agencies.

To find internet sights and related searches offering both written and video exercises information attuned to different age groups go to.

Exercises for seniors (add age) years Example Exercise for seniors 70 years.

Mall walking is a popular year-round exercise and possible social event if in the vicinity of an enclosed mall with available regular transportation individually or in a group to the location. Bicycling for fit seniors is an option as is park, trail and street walking but they are dependent on season and weather conditions. During inclement weather a temporary walking option may be to mentally plan a route in the home with enough laps to maintain the bases of the exercise routine. A permanent or back-up walking exercise plan if space is available and finances allow for an inexpensive or used basic treadmill or indoor bike that will suffice for year-round exercise no matter the season.

Workout gyms can be ideal for younger and fit seniors but for older seniors most gyms by design are not older senior friendly because of the heavy muscular requirement of the workout equipment, social atmosphere and most important lack of individual monitoring for signs of distress. Over exercise, trying to keep up with the Jones, is a heighten possibility with lifelong competitive seniors and can lead to muscle or back injuries and heart stress when exercising is pushed outside of appropriate age limits.

Exercise for seniors is not muscle building but for body maintenance, weight management and the slowing of natural body muscle degeneration by positive physical activity and is a form of preventive medicine.

Many senior citizens centers offer moderate facilities for workouts. But most do not have experienced staff to aid in the management of the overall workout. Management of the exercise regimen to include the number of repetitions, weight and speed limitations for a safe program is the responsibility of the exerciser. All exercises should begin in moderation and only increase in intensity in small increments that do not cause an after affect.

Upon establishing of a personal feel good after and fitness goal matching exercise regimen based on a moderate level of physical abilities should be sanctioned, reviewed and monitored by the primary care physician or a physical therapist and documented as a workable plan. Especially if a gym workout is involved.

47

WHAT SENIORS NEED TO KNOW ABOUT MEDICAL ADVERTISEMENTS

The constant bombardment of commercials from television, radio, pop-up internet advertisements, direct mailings, robot phone calls and flyer handouts promoting a medical breakthrough or new procedure, home use medical devices, diets, ointments, cure all medications and vitamins can be confusing. The advertisements are directed toward individuals that may or may not be currently receiving medical treatments or to those having similar symptoms marketed in the advertised affliction. The volume of information and medical language can be overwhelming to seniors and difficult to surmise if it will be beneficial to personal wellness.

Advertising claims from major pharmaceutical companies and legitimate medical providers do accurately portray symptoms and the possibility of a wellness improvement depending on the condition and stage of the affliction. Awareness of symptoms and cures through advertisements can benefit seniors to recognize a possible previously unknown onset or better cure for an affliction. Precaution is needed when self-diagnosing the advertised symptoms; and not to confuse or overreact to normal aging events and a physician's previously diagnosed illness symptoms. The primary care physician should always be consulted for an opinion prior to incorporating additional non-prescription remedies or devices into a wellness health regiment.

Beware of advertising claims that may be overselling their products by inflating the curability of their medications and the need for medical devices. The internet has reborn the charlatan medicine man and his elixirs and gadgets of the past. Formulas may not contain suitable ingredients or enough dosages causing no positive effect on an affliction. Be vigilant of unrecognized brands or me to copies of the medications ordered online. Do not open the door to incorrect medicating and possible other ailments from imitation medical products. Ordering products from known accredited vendors or direct from the manufacturer is always the safest way to handle online medical purchases. Side effect of any medication should always be a concern and discussed with the primary care physician.

Diet programs as advertised on television and other forms of advertising are directed to young and middle age individuals. Diets offering prepared meals and those with specific foods and servings may not be ideal for seniors. Involvement in a strict diet regiment can deprive a senior of nutritional needs and lead to possible nourishment and vitamin deficiencies. If a diet is deemed necessary for one's wellness a program with proper nourishment should only be instigated and monitored under the direction of a certified dietitian. Each individual senior based on physical being and afflictions require a different balance of nutrition's and vitamins than a one fits all diet offers. See Topic: Natural Food Nutrition for more information.

Consideration for the use of advertised medical devices whether exercise or wellbeing should be based on bodily strength capabilities, clinical treatment needs and ability to improve the overall medical regiment. Purchase without the input of the primary care physician of devices that cannot be safely and beneficially used because of an affliction could be harmful and is a waste of money.

GENERAL WELL BEING MANAGEMENT

TEETH – VISION – HEARING – FEET – SKIN – SLEEP

The following are comments and suggested methods for detection and management of repetitive non-life-threatening body welfare issues.

TEETH - Oral hygiene is important for overall wellness and is an established preventive measure to poor health. Ignoring daily dental care can lead to cavities, gum disease (Gingivitis - Periodontal Infection), oral surgery and is a cause of bacterial build up in the gums, on the teeth and in the mouth lining that can be absorbed into the respiratory and digestive systems and be carried though out the body in the blood stream possibly causing infections and aggravating current health issues.

Establish a relationship with a dental practice by creating a routine of a minimum of two visits per year. Oral health problems are magnified with aging requiring not only the normal inspection for tooth decay or loose fillings and the cleaning to eliminate plaque and tartar but need to include visual checks by the dental hygienist and/or dentist for mouth sores, red and puffy or bleeding gums, loose teeth and signs of mouth cancer that are not normally addressed by the primary care physician. Preparation for a dental appointment needs to include a reminder list of visual checks to be performed and notes on any abnormalities noticed since last visit.

It is recommended that using a flossing handled device reduces the amount of dexterity need to floss the teeth properly or a flossing water pick can also be used. An electric toothbrush is also recommended for seniors because of the effortlessness of maneuverability around and between teeth, gum massaging and degree of cleanness achieved.

Oral issues like dry mouth that in most cases is caused by medications is uncomfortable, can exacerbate bacteria build up and can cause cavities is easily contained with a dry mouth moisturizing rinse as needed and at bedtime.

Oral inhaler users for various pulmonary issues need to after each use gargle with water or mouth wash to prevent buildup of chemical residue on the gums and between teeth that could promote taste changes, lesions and bacterial growth.

Apprehension by some seniors of dental procedures is rooted in youth experiences. Dental practices and specialty dental procedures have advanced to the degree of almost if not completely painless and with medications to hasten healing.

VISION – An annual vision screening with an Ophthalmologists (certified for surgery) or Optometrists is encouraged for senior citizens. Aging can and does cause deterioration of vision that can require new or changes to current corrective lenses. A full screening for the possibility of eye disease common to seniors along with the physician being made aware of past vision history, current eyesight and general eye problems at the biannual appointment. If a negative eye event occurs treat it as any medical emergency and go to the emergency room or set a soonest emergency appointment with the physician.

One of the many diseases associated with older seniors is Age-Related Macular Degeneration (AMD) a distortion of the retinas light sensitive membrane at the back of the eye which causes straight on blurred vision which can grow larger or become a blank spot further obscuring sight, reading ability and fine details. In most patients a one eye at a time self-wellness test of waviness in sharp vertical and horizontal lines i.e. line grid or solid edges of a door or window frame would be an indication to be further tested for AMD. Both eyes can be affected and if not medical treated can lead to blindness of the affected eye. A senior should be tested a least once a year for AMD onset.

Glaucoma is vision loss due to fluid buildup in the eyeball with symptoms of pain and headache behind the eyeball, blurred vision, halos around bright lights, tunnel vision, eye redness and swelling. Once diagnosed eye drops on a rigid schedule or minor surgery to drain the fluid are available to reduce or eliminate the affliction. The treatment decision to be determined by the Ophthalmologists based on the progression of the disease.

A cataract is an opaque film spot that blocks eyesight and can be replaced surgically with artificial implant. In seniors it can be found in varying degrees in both eyes. It is important for the Ophthalmologists to use the corrective lens suited to the patients' needs and placed in proper location. Because of the seriousness of an eye surgery it is recommended that a second opinion be sought as to the correctness of the calculation used to determine the type and location of the implant.

Over the counter eye drops for minor irritations, if not chronic, such as dry and watery eyes, redness from strain, swollen and itching are available from the local pharmacy. If irritations persist, contact a physician.

Over the counter vision correction glasses come with various lens powers to aid a farsighted individual to pick the best power for reading. They are at best an inexpensive short-term alternative for younger individuals experiencing there initial first hard to read event and not a recommended solution for seniors. It must be considered that each eye is different and lens powers may vary from eye to eye. If lens powers are not properly balanced additional strain can be put upon the eyes causing additional deterioration to sight. The over the counter vision glasses are not an alternative to a complete eye screening especially for senior citizens.

After bathing do not rub eye area to dry it can cause a spike in eye pressure and be harmful to or create chronic eye problems. Pat gently until dry.

HEARING – Age related hearing loss unless associated with a major event i.e. accidental or medical, is normally a gradual change. One obvious sign of hearing lost is Tinnitus (ringing in the ear/s). As the hearing loss gradually increases over time higher and higher audio adjustments on the television or other devices are made with request to individuals to repeat or speak louder. Additionally, request from other to speak lower are signs of reduced hearing capacity. One possible problem may be excessive harden ear wax in the ear canal causing reduced hearing that needs to be removed carefully or by a medical professional. When loud audio devices, missed comments and loud speech makes it difficult to connect with others and becomes the norm it is now time to have a hearing test.

If the primary care physician does not have the capabilities to do an in-office hearing test there are major hearing aid companies that have maul stores who will do it for free. There are also hearing test that can be done online but due require ear headphones to evaluate properly. A consultation with a doctor of Audiology (hearing specialist) to get detailed testing along with current need and future loss profile is recommended to evaluate any initial test preformed prior to any purchase hearing aids. Minor initial loss of hearing in one or both ears may not always require expensive hearing aids initially. Type of and when hearing aids are needed should be discussed with the Audiologist and a plan for implantation reflecting expectations and cost established.

FEET - Feet can be an indicator of wellness and should continually be self-monitored for changes. Long term swollen feet can be associated with a wide range of major health issues such as heart, kidney, liver, vein thrombosis problems, gout and obesity to name a few. Short term water gain bloating can be caused by drugs like steroids, prolong positional inactivity and lack of walking exercise. A simple visual observation along with a pressure test of placing a thumb below and to the front of the ankle or atop of the foot can indicate bloating caused by water build up or reduction status. All bloating or swelling of the feet should immediately be evaluated by the primary care physician to determine if a medication, undiagnosed medical issue or an increase in a previous diagnosis is the cause.

Foot pain can have many causes such as nerve problems or the need for specialized footwear and should be evaluated by a Podiatrist (foot doctor) initially to determine the next pain management procedural course of action and treatment if necessary. Other foot disorders such as ingrown toenails, funguses, athlete's foot, broken or dislocated toes, heel spurs, blisters, bunions, corn and calluses or any foot problems should be treated by a Podiatrist. There are over the counter cures for some of the basic ailments i.e. fungus, athlete's foot, blisters, bunions and corns for self-treatment. Seniors should consult with a Podiatrist for most effective cures before self-medicating.

Self-clipping of toenails for some seniors because of weight, reach, eyesight or back problems cannot safely and accurately be accomplished. If no friendly help is available, the local nail salon can accomplish the task with or without a full pedicure.

SKIN – Most skin problems among seniors are a normal part of aging like dry skin can be managed by over the counter medications. Persistent skin issues can indicate the possibility of damage or disease to the skin layers or underlying wellness problems. The primary care physician and a Dermatologist should be consulted for proper evaluation and treatment of all skin ailments.

There are three types of skin cancers associated with aging Melanoma, Basal & Squamous cell skin cancers primarily associated with seniors with Melanoma being the most common. Factors for skin cancer are over exposure to natural sun, artificial UV light and hereditary history. White skinned, freckled, red or blond hair and blue eye people being at the highest risk. Warning signs are moles and groups of moles that change color, size and shape with irregular edges. Further skin disturbances such as ulcers, change of pigmentation of skin areas and sever itching and bleeding. All are signs of possible onset of skin cancer and a Dermatologist should be consulted immediately for testing. Treatments are available depending on the extent of the cancer to include surgery, drugs and radiation that can be used to control and heal preventing a life-threatening event.

The dark skin spot condition normally referred to as liver spots have nothing to do with liver functions. Skin spots are a normal nonreversible condition of aging skin caused by UV exposure over the years. Seniors can reduce additional dark skin spots when outdoors by using a sun block ointment and cover exposed areas to prevent direct UV contact with the skin.

Minor small dry, flaky and itchy skin areas are a normal part of aging and the discomfort can be reduced with the use of a moisturizer formulated for dry skin on a daily basis. Adjustment of bathing schedules to every other day to allow natural oils to lubricate the skin can also help. Further, the wearing of loose-fitting cotton clothing in lieu of synthetic fabrics is all part of being comfortable by reducing itching from dryness.

Rashes and there are many different varieties some of the most common are Psoriasis that causes surface areas to crack or split, thicken, redden, become scaly or blister with small pimple like pustules. Drug related rashes are normally associated with antibiotics and anticonvulsants medications. Other common rashes such as Eczema (untreated dry skin), Contact Dermatitis (allergic or unclean contact transfer), Hives (allergies to medications or foods) and Scabies (infestation of mites) are the major rashes that afflict the senior population. Obviously, there are more skin rashes with some that could be an indication of an underlying medical problem. All rashes especially persistent rashes should always be evaluated by the primary care physician and a Dermatologist.

Bruises in seniors because of the more fragile blood vessels and thinning skin can occur with only minor bumping or scraping causing the blood vessels to rupture creating the bruise pattern. Apply a cold compress to the bruised area to reduce size, inflammation and promote healing.

SLEEP – For senior citizens to maintain daily health and activities a nightly sleeping pattern should be implemented with a regular bedtime which relaxes the body into a sleep mode. The number of hours of sleep required by each individual varies but should be in the range of seven to eight hours per night for those over 65 along with a moderate daily nap are important to maintain a well-balanced rested body. Napping in the evening in front of the TV should be avoided since it can unbalance the bodies sleep mode and cause sleep time awaking during the night. Recurring lack of sleep can affect the immune system, create memory loss and inability to concentration, be prone to accidents and tiredness i.e. yawning and disinterest in activities. If chronic pain is an issue that prevents falling into or maintain a normal sleep pattern consult the primary care physician for treatment.

Basic self-treatments to adjust for minor sleep deprivation are to avoid caffeine, smoking and alcohol at bedtime. Further avoid bright lights, large heavy meals or snacks a few hours before bedtime and have a friendly sleep environment i.e. quietness, comfortable bedding, pleasant environments, relaxing sleep position, pleasant or non-existent smells and proper regulated room temperature.

Insomnia is a serious sleep deprivation problem even if only a few nights a week and can cause inability to fall asleep, stark awakenings during the night, fatigue, mood swings, clumsiness, confusion, distorted memory, depression, decreased mental capabilities, aggravate current medical conditions and lead to mental disorders. Further due to the bodies reduced immune system from lack of enough sleep other medical issues can arise. The primary care physician or a sleep specialist should be consulted and a program for treatment established.

Sleep Apnea is a serious condition where unknowingly and unawake the sleeper stops breathing a number of times per hour during the night causing reduced oxygen into the blood stream. Sleep apnea creates symptoms of extreme fatigue, loud snoring, headaches, memory loss, depression, chocking and gasping during sleep, weight gain, sore throat and if unattended the possibility of cardiovascular disease along with the other ailments associated with lack of proper sleep. Fortunately sleep apnea is controllable. A test to determine the severity of the problem can be performed by a sleep specialist in an overnight controlled environment or can be conducted at home using a small portable testing apparatus. Once the severity of the sleep apnea is determined a small breathing apparatus called a CPAP is programmed to be used on a bedside table with enough tubing connected to an adjustable face mask to allow for various comfortable sleep positions. The process reduces the number of breathing stoppages to a clinical acceptable rate allowing for a normal sleep pattern. Over the counter sleeping aids will not cure or reduce a sleep apnea problem. Discuss with the primary care physician his recommendation of a sleep specialist.

Prior to the use of over the counter sleeping aids contact the primary care physician for evaluation of the brand of sleeping pills, possible effect on current medication and if safe to use, how often and a recommendation on dosage amount. Keep a record of usage and if effective as an aid for a full nights uninterrupted sleep.

Nightmares can be associated with sleep apnea, anxiety, depression, sleep deprivation, PTSD (Post Traumatic Stress Disorder), medication and dosage changes, withdrawal from substances i.e. alcohol or psychological drugs and even with late night snacks or meals especially if spicy. Nightmares and night terrors can also be associated with traumatic experiences such as an accident or an actual or conceived attach on one's person. Unrealized events or thoughts occurring during the waking hours can create subconscious triggers for nightmares during the hours of sleep. Night terrors are not usually remembered other than upon awaking with a feeling of unknown terror. Most if not all nightmares occur during REM (Rapid Eye Movement) sleep in the early morning hours with only, if at all, disconnected portions remembered.

Constantly reoccurring nightmares with the help of the primary care physician can possibly be controlled with evaluation and changes of current medications and dosages with side effects that affect sleep to possibly include medications to reduce bouts of anxiety and depression as part of the treatment. A recommendation if changes to and additional medications do not reduce the nightmare cycle additional assistance by a sleep therapist with a comprehensives program should be the next step. It is important for a senior to have a comfortable, fear free night of restful sleep to maintain wellness.

HOSPITAL ADMITTANCE

There are three types of hospital admittances which are Emergency Room, Outpatient and Inpatient.

EMERGENCY ROOM has two ways to be formally admitted. The first is by ambulance with emergency personal in attendance with no time for the patient to prepare. The carrying and presentation at the soonest opportunity to the medical staff by the patient or accompanying individual of the second condensed list of medication and information as outlined in the Topic Listing and Control of Medications is important. The list especially of major ailments will aid the medical staff in selecting appropriate emergency treatment when possible that does not adversely affect current medical conditions.

The second emergency room admittance is by self-admitting with a narrow window of time to prepare. The second condensed list of medication and any other pertinent information such as abusive and current alcohol or illicit drug use should be relayed to the emergency room admitting staff or attending medical staff to be included into the patient's computerized chart prior to treatment. Proper information will allow the medical staff to make informed decisions on treatment best suited for the patient's situation. At time of sign-in the patient will be put into a waiting room queue that can constantly change based on the severity of new critical emergencies. The patient if self-admitting should be aware that an extended stay as an inpatient could occur depending on the prognoses of the event and should be prepared mentally for such a possibility.

OUTPATIENT medical treatments are by appointment and require a check-in with the administrative staff. At most hospitals treatments include special radiology and diagnostic imaging, chemotherapy, radiation therapy, post-surgical checkups, rehabilitation physical therapy to name a few that require a in hospital or hospital associate setting to perform with confidence of results. A procedure or minor surgery requiring anesthesia to be administered and monitored by an anesthesiologist should always be performed in a hospital setting. Phone contact by a hospital representative using the hospital protocol instructions as how to prepare for each type of procedure such as a timetable for food, liquid and medicine intake prior to appointment arrival must be strictly adhered to especially for surgery that require anesthesia. Further pre surgery or procedure information from other physicians as to physical conditions such as heart status, physical stamina, lung disorder complications and other conditions based on personal history may be requested by the performing physician to include additional or up to date testing of afflictions for evaluation. After check-in that will require a photo ID, insurance and Medicare information the patient will be escorted to a cubical where pre-surgery or procedure preparations by nursing staff will occur to include questions of current wellbeing, the adherence to pre-surgery or procedure instructions, review of medications, alcohol and illicit drug usage and long term medical issues. This is where the second condensed written medication list and informational listing as outlined in the Topic Listing and Control of Medications will be of great assistance. Failure to disclose all medical history prior to a procedure can cause additional problems during and after a medical procedure. Test of blood pressure, glucose level, possible EKG and other testing requested by the physician will be performed. A single IV with secondary portals will be inserted into the arm as a pathway for fluids such as saline or medication fluid drips, pre-anesthesia relaxing drug may be introduced also with portals readily available for any emergency medical need. Prior to the procedure or surgery, the performing physician and anesthesiologist will visit to discuss the medical procedure and answer any questions. After the medical procedure and movement to a recovery monitoring area until awake and recovering within the parameters set by the physician. A visit by the performing physician to explain the results of the procedure and future expectations for recovery or additional medical procedures to be undertaken will be discussed. Once it is determined that the patient has met the parameters of full recovery and administrative paper work is completed to include instructions by the nursing staff at time of discharge as to physical and food intake restriction and date of a follow up visit are given the patient will be escorted by wheelchair and discharged at curb side from the hospital.

INPATIENT status is considered to be a one or more-night stay in the hospital. The necessity for a hospital admittance stay can be for major surgery, emergency room admittance for physical injuries, emergency room diagnoses to include signs of the possibility of a heart attack, admission by physicians order for a major illness and further evaluation and testing, infections, pulmonary problems i.e. pneumonia and monitoring of yet to be determined medical issues.

The hospital will have in place protocols for all inpatient entries from the emergency room and transfers from other hospitals. The administration staff, when appropriate, will process and explain to the patient and family, in the patient's room, all necessary insurance and hospital signature required paperwork. The attending physician/s and nursing staff will explain to the patient and family the diagnosis, procedures and expectations.

Patients to undergo planned surgery will be based on urgency of need, scheduling between the hospital and surgeons' staff, anesthesiologist and operation room nursing staff availability. Further pre surgery collection of information from the primary care physician and other entities as to overall physical conditions, latest EKG and heart evaluation by a heart specialist, physical stamina status condition, lung disorder complications and other conditions based on personal history will be requested by the performing physician to include additional and updated testing for evaluation. Once a date and time is established for the surgery and just prior to the surgery the patient will be contacted by phone by a hospital representative using the hospital protocol surgery preparation requirements for the procedure such as time line for food, liquid, medication intake and any other special instructions prior to admittance. The instructions need to be exactly followed as prescribed. Failure to fully follow pre surgery instructions can cause the surgery to be canceled or by not relaying breaches of instructions when asked by the nursing staff could create complications during or post-surgery.

After check-in with the administration staff that will require a photo ID, insurance and Medicare information the patient will be escorted to a pre operation cubical where pre-surgery preparations by nursing staff will be performed. Questions concerning current occurring pain, general wellbeing, the adherence to pre-surgery instructions, review of medications, use of alcohol and illicit drugs and long-term medical issues. The second condensed written mediation list and informational listing as outlined in the Topic Listing and Control of Medications will greatly assist informational input into the patients' electronic chart. Test of blood pressure, glucose level, possible EKG and other testing requested by physician will be performed. A single IV with secondary portals will be inserted into the arm to be available for pre surgery, surgery and post-surgery medications and be readily available for any emergency surgical need. Fluid IV drip that may include saline, antibiotics or other medications prescribed by the attending physician and a pre-anesthesia relaxing drug may be introduced depending on the procedure. Prior to the surgery the performing physician and anesthesiologist will visit to discuss the procedures and answer any questions. After surgery the patient will be transferred to ICU or a recovery area depending on the seriousness of the surgery for monitoring until awake and functioning with no adverse effect or trauma attributed to the surgery that may require special treatment or addition surgical intervention. Upon a release from ICU by the performing physician the patient will be transferred to a hospital room for additional monitoring and recovery. Once the patient has recovery sufficiently the performing physician will visit and discuss the surgery or procedure and future expectations for recovery or additional medical steps to be undertaken to bring about full wellness. The patient's medical fitness for discharge will be determined by the attending physician instructions for the transfer from hospital to home recovery. Discharge paperwork will be processed and the prescriptions for medications for recovery will be issued at this time. Final discharge will occur at curbside to which the patient will be escorted by wheelchair.

Home recovery from surgery or major illness requiring additional care will involve home based appointments with a visiting nurse and a physical therapist to monitor the patient's post event progress and overall physical wellbeing. An inspection of the patients living and recovery areas by the nurse based on current medical status to include suggestions, if applicable, as to what may need to be done to upgrade the areas in the home that will create a safe environment during and after recovery. Further assistance will include the scheduling of the intake of medication prescribed post-surgery or necessary for the continued treatment of the illness to include previously prescribed medications by the primary care physician. Assistance by the nurse will include organizing medications for daily intake into a weekly day and nighttime pill box, evaluation of incision/s healing, change bandages as applicable and alleviate post procedure stress though compassion. The physical therapist will conduct therapy sessions and create an exercise program to be used daily between the therapist visits. The exercise program will be based on the specific therapeutic needs of post-surgery or major illness recovery using a protocol designed that encompasses the specialized exercises needed. The number of appointments will depend on the progress of the patient, ability to self-monitor and release by the attending physician.

Anxiety prior to hospital admittance is a common occurrence. It is unlikely that a relaxant will be prescribed to a patient prior to admittance. If admitted for a procedure or surgery as an outpatient or inpatient that requires anesthesia it is very likely that the anesthesiologist will order a mild relaxant to be put into the IV drip during preparation for the procedure. The best way to deal with the anxiety of future unknowns of a medical procedure or surgery is not to dwell on the possibility of a negative outcome. One must mental view all the positive aspects that will result from the cure, repair and recovery from a medical issue that will increase the quality of life. Further view any specialized testing or non-evasive procedure to be performed prior to hospitalization without anxiety as a possibility of conformation of a future non-medical event or as the early diagnosis of the need for additional medical attention and direction. A programmed treatment of a now known medical problem with all the resources of the medical community will be directed to alleviate or eliminate the diagnosis. Relief from anxiety is knowledge.

To simplify admittance into the hospital for a procedure that will require the wearing of a hospital gown or partial disrobing, dress in easily removal clothing and shoes that can also make redressing less physical stressful. Carry a list of all medication, medical history information, photo identification and insurance information to aid in the admission process. Leave all jewelry and valuables at home in a safe place when being admitted for either an outpatient or inpatient procedure. Secure reliable transportation to and from the hospital.

Do not carry daily medications needs into the hospital as an inpatient. The hospital pharmacy will supply the patient's normal daily needs based on the attending physician's recommendation during the hospital stay.

It is important, if one chooses, to have available at time of admission or on file at the hospital an Advance Directive for the final decision if the patient is incapable of voicing the desire for the stoppage of medical treatment. Forms can be found online by entering the search words Medical Advance Directive.

SENIOR ABUSE

This topic does not deal with physical abuse since a senior citizen living independently will have the mental capability and physical ability to alleviate the threat or contact authorities.

Fortunately, most senior citizens have a support network of immediate and extended family to include friends and paid caregivers when applicable to provide support and assistance. Others may not be as fortunate with a limited or no network, modest finances and may only have social services and senior center daytime facilities for support.

All independent seniors no matter their financial status, need to be aware to protect their resources of a budgeted fixed income no matter the level of retirement lifestyle from the possibility of prescription over pricing, being taken advantage by others or fraud.

Prescription drug cost can vary greatly depending on types of medical insurance, amount of the co-pay required, and pharmacy programmed price for a medication. Do not except an initial expensive pharmacy charge for a medication without contacting Medicare and/or the main or secondary insurance provider to aid in the reduction of the initial cost.

The primary care physician's office should also be able to assist. Surprising what a few phone calls can accomplish.

The most prevalent drain on retirement resources is requests for monies from individuals that are using the seniors loving vulnerability to help others and past generosity to gain access to funds. Seniors should not use the limited resources needed to maintain current retirement lifestyle to support financial loan requests. Savings set aside for future expenses and emergencies should never be loaned and the senior should never co-sign a note for anything. In most cases the recipient, no matter what is promised may not be able to or from the start has no intentions of paying back the loan. It is difficult to say no when it is a family member or a close friend that is asking. The best way to step away from the pressure of saying no or being pressed to say yes is to tell the individual that all financial expenditures are made by an accountant, lawyer or protective dominate relative who they will need to contact for an answer. May be a little white lie, may be true or be a previously arranged answer of no. This will normally stop any frivols request for funds. If it is determined that the loan is justified to relieve an immediate major short-term financial crisis to a close family member and finances are available without compromising the current retirement lifestyle. It should be discussed with an accountant or lawyer as to the feasibility of the loan and depending on the amount of monies involved proper promissory paperwork with a payback schedule, penalties and possible property lien should be signed prior to any funds being transferred. If they are not willing to sign for the loan it is likely they did not have intentions of repaying.

Attempts to control or obtain property by immoral means perpetrated on well-meaning and unsuspecting senior citizens can come in many forms and in some cases from individuals least likely to be suspected of taking advantage of the senior citizen.

The senior citizen should never without advice from an attorney and accountant sign away any real estate, business interest, stocks and bonds or any income generating investments to any person or entity. In some financial situation there could be a tax benefit, business management necessity or personal reasons for the signing over management control of finances or property ownership. Prior to any signed agreement a legal binding contract generated by an attorney that assures financial payment, right to audit records if not a finalized purchase and pre-defined legal recourse and penalties for breach of contract by receiving party.

There are abusive financial scams both small and large designed especially for and purposely directed at seniors and come from many directions to include telemarketers, door knockers selling questionable products or services, request for a donation from dubious charities and unneeded, incorrect or sloppily done home repairs. Just say no or as previously recommended in this topic and tell them all financial expenditures are approved and made by another.

When work is needed for home repairs or upgrades to increase a senior's comfort or mobility always deal with an accredited, established, licensed and bonded local contractor. A binding and written signed agreement as to the exact scope of work to be done that includes all final associated cost of labor, materials and permit fees. Start and finish dates should be a part of the contract with a penalty for late or non-completion. Be sure to discuss what inconveniences and for how long could occur. Only a nominal down payment to schedule work should be made. Additional progress intermittent payments and the final payment should not be made until all work in each and the final stage is competed and meets with expectations.

When contracting for maid or home medical service providers a written agreement as to the exact cost, scope of services to be performed with each visit. Background checks should be supplied by the bonded service provider as to the identity of individuals entering the home.

Protection of and recovery is limited for items that become missing from the home which may not be discovered for days or weeks making it impossible to connect with a visit. If discovered immediately and can be connected to a specific visit contact should be made with employers of any service personal suspected. Pointing a finger at a wrong doer can create repercussion both legal and internal family complication when a family member is suspected. Finding unquestionable solid proof without catching someone in the act or with secretive interior and exterior video surveillance will be difficult to prove unless items are discovered in their possession. Without unquestionable proof as an individual seeking justice be wary of repercussions. If of enough value do not hesitate in contacting authorities, insurance company and dominate family member concerning the missing items and suspicions with any evidence to aid in possible recovery. Recovery of items may be next to impossible unless voluntarily returned under pressure or recovered by the authorities. Do not be influenced or confused by someone stating that the item/s have been gone for a very long time, given away or were never there. It is best to document by being proactive to protect against items disappearing by using current phone technology to photograph all valuables to include jewelry, family heirlooms and generalized pictures taken of each room which will also help with any insurance claim and estate settlements. Make all visitors and service providers aware that dated photographs of everything in the home have been taken.

After shopping or just periodically check banking information for credit card and especially debit card transactions for unauthorized use. When contracted assistance is employed in the home secure all cash, valuable jewelry, credit and debit cards and written pin numbers in a secure area.

Do not open the door to be used or abused by becoming involved with other people's personal problems especially those that include disputes between children, relatives or friends. It will never end well. Simply relate to the parties that making judgments of other problems would be personally unsettling. Further stating it is not appropriate to discuss the situation and it is inappropriate to be asked to take sides. Taking sides, no matter who is right or wrong would put one in the middle of a dispute upsetting a comfortable, unencumbered and un-stressful retirement lifestyle. Politely pass on making any comments or the taking of sides.

SENIOR LIVING ARRANGEMENTS

Senior independent retirement communities vary greatly depending on one's financial ability, desired location and type of amenities. An independent living retirement community is fine for those seniors with the finical assets to buy into and with enough retirement income to afford additional monthly maintenance fees associated with the purchased condo or home. For those seniors who are not interested in major amenities i.e. golf, tennis etc. and are not willing to finically support actives they would not or physical could not participate in. It becomes a choice between an upscale community with major amenities and a moderate cost range retirement community with lower monthly maintenance fees that offers independent living space, dining, game and meeting rooms or maintaining current lifestyle living arrangements in current home. Relocation to an independent lifestyle community will not only require downsizing it may not be in one's best interest based on cost. In home living with enough assistance for basic needs like maid service, bill paying assistance, grocery delivery, available transportation and restaurant meal delivery with the ability to dine out with family and friends may be less expensive than a senior citizens community even with the household upkeep expenses.

There are seniors who do not want to leave the feelings of security, the comfort of a home of many years and be away from lifelong neighbors, friends and relatives. Additionally, being familiar with the general area makes running errands, shopping and traveling to appointments a known commodity.

The following is for those who do not want to leave the home and those who are now living on a limited income or both.

Household living arrangements for independent seniors can be varied and should always be based on proximity and relationship with immediate family, individual needs and finances to determine a course of action. Depending on age and medical necessities there are local senior centers that can be visited for activates. If home care is needed a senior care agency can schedule daily or full-time live-in caregivers to assist for a fee. Assistance can also be obtained from government sponsored local senior social services agencies to schedule a visiting professional caregiver several days or more a week to assist with medical, transportation or personal issues at no cost. Alert devices can also be used for emergency issues when alone.

The most advantages and practical alternative is sharing the home with a relative or bona fide friend within the same age group, with similar circumstances and interest capable of assisting with living expenses. The balance of mutual assistance and a caring relationship can make for a more enjoyable senior lifestyle.

Beware of squatters abusing the home. What is a squatter? A squatter is person or persons who have established a residence in the home taking advantage of the senior citizens good will without compensation. The senior can be put in an awkward position by a freeloading relative seeking a place to live who in many cases has been evicted by others for lack of financial responsibility. A dominate relative or friend should be consulted as to the reputation and motives of the individual and feasibility of such a relationship that will affect current standard of lifestyle. The senior must take into consideration the loss of privacy, adjusting to the possibility of an imposed lifestyle and increases to the fixed limited retirement budget i.e. electricity use, water usage, toiletries to include paper products and biggest of all the food budget increase.

If after consultation with others and budget review the senior citizen makes a compassionate decision to temporarily assist an individual certain household rules need to be established in writing and signed. To include a nonnegotiable move out date and immediate eviction for lack of employment if capable, failure to aid with financial support, rowdiness to include loud music, sleepover visitors, illegal activities, poor personal hygiene, failure to reimburses and other activates deemed a nuisance added to the agreement by the senior citizen. Further the individual is to assist with household chores, maintain a clean allotted personal living space and reimburse for the increased living expenses generated with a previously agree upon dollar amount paid weekly until the move out date. In some state and local governments laws may exist that if an individual resides in a home for a specified period they cannot be evicted. Therefore, a signed contract is important.

On the other hand, if the senior citizen becomes a tenant an agreement in writing as to living arrangements to include a pre-established rental amount needs to be agreed upon and signed. If a decision is made to share expenses, then both parties must understand the associated cost and there responsibility in writing. Household duties, privileges and limitations with an understanding of the distribution of cost of groceries based on shared meals or if independent meals to include refrigerator storage and kitchen cabinets space availability must be part of the agreement.

The wrong choice of a full-time long term live-in incompatible companion can make for a miserable and financially stressful retirement lifestyle. Be sure of the background, intentions and mental stability of any possible individual being considered to share the retirement years and living space with.

TRAVEL

Young and fit seniors will not have or only minor problems with any type of travel for visitation, vacations, viewing or playing in sporting events and day or overnight trips. The following does not fully apply to this senior group except for some commonsense steps to prevent possible travel issues and problems.

The restrictions of age and medical condition can greatly affect older and ailing senior citizen travel to include type of transportation, length of stay, travel stress, medication intake, device use requirements and ability to move about at a personal pace.

The most convent long distance method of transportation for capable drivers is the automobile for moderate daily travel distances up to 250 miles depending on the driver's fortitude. The second is a choice between train or bus travel depending on station locations and the practicality of travel to and availability of transportation upon arrival. The most difficult and stressful for an older senior is air travel. When extreme distances are involved air travel may not be avoidable and should be approached with preparation, awareness of difficulties and possible need of assistance.

Automobile travel is the most convenient for the following reasons. Adjustable departure and arrival times, no special packing or carrying luggage for distances with heavy medical devices, one time loading of necessities, establishment of personal pace, comfort and ability to make as needed meal, rest and bathroom stops including the ability to breakup the travel distance with an overnight stay at a motel or hotel. Further and most important is the ability to carry and use all needed medical supplies without restrictions to include respiratory specialty apparatus to assist breathing and sleep, electronic devices to monitor conditions required to conduct evaluation and to maintain wellness with the additional space for a wheelchair, braces, walking supports and any personal specialty items without explanation or stranger inspection.

If overnight stops during the trip are part of the schedule, simply pack items that will be need for the stopover separately for accessibility for minimal unloading of the vehicle.

After unloading with only the nights necessities re-park the vehicle in the lighted area in front of the motel or hotel entrance for security.

The flexibility of automobile travel allows for adjustment of a departure date for a longer or shorter visit.

Train and bus travel is not as convenient as automobile and if not express can have a number of stops and possible transfers but does relieve the stress and fatigue of driving distances. It is most practical for large city urban dwellers traveling from one major city to another. It does allow for the senior to carry sufficient medical necessities i.e. medicines and devices without restrictions. It however does require proper packing of all items and some toting at time of boarding and arrival.

Air travel can be stressful not only in preparation, but the full experience of the fast pace needed for check in, processing through a TSA (Transportation Security Administration) security check point, travel to departure gate, boarding and dealing with the impoliteness' of others during the seating process. Upon arrival at a destination the rush to deplane by others, long treks to baggage pick-up area if applicable, recovery of baggage from luggage carousel and an additional trek out of the secure area to meet assistance or to curbside for a prearranged pick-up. Except for check-in prior to entering the secure area of the airport and leaving the secure area at destination a passenger must tote personal items and carry-on luggage unless senior citizen disability assistance arrangements are made with the airline.

The airline/s to be traveled can be contacted for special senior citizen assistance with wheelchair or motorized rides to departure and from arrival gates. It may require waiting but well worth it. Upon arrival at the airport either at the check-in counter or from a uniformed employee of the airline to be traveled always request the assistances promised.

Preparations for travel for a senior citizen with or without a wellness issues requires establishing a check list that can vary depending of mode of transportation.

Basic reminder list:
• Contact primary care physician as to the feasibility and restriction of travel and mode of travel. Things to be considered related to air travel are the health hazards because of the close quarters of an airline cabin can be devastating to a senior citizen. Health hazards can range from reduced air pressure and oxygen effecting COPD suffers, tight

and long-term uncomfortable seating causing joint stiffness or blood clots in the legs and exposure to foreign airborne or physical contact illnesses that a senior's immune system may not be able to cope with. All aspects of travel health hazards and the possibility of the inability to use medical devices because of use restriction or lack of available space to be considered. Based on the senior's current wellness condition a medical decision or advice with recommendations as to restrictions, ways to avoid health hazards and travel mode need to be discussed and implemented prior to senior citizen travel.

• Prepare medications: Reference Topic: Listing and Control of Medications and carry schedule to include physician contact information on one's person for emergencies.

• Adjustment of medication time intake timetable if time zone changes are involved in consultation with primary care physician.

• Carry several extra days of medications beyond the planned stay.

• Prepare a list of medical devices that will be needed with carry bags.

• If extended stay prior to leaving contact pharmacy to refill any prescriptions that do not have enough medication for the length of the stay.

• Make arrangements for a house sitter or watcher to collect mail and newspapers and make periodic interior walk through inspections if no one else is living in the home.

• Leave a dated itinerary with home companion, family or a friend to include phone contact numbers of the location to be visited i.e. family, friends, resort and overnight hotel or motel intended stays.

• Carry independently of wallet credit card numbers and card company cancelation call numbers to immediately cancel loss or stolen credit cards.

• Do not openly expose excessive cash on one's person when traveling. Carry only what will be needed for a day or two to make purchases with the balance being hidden. If paying in cash, with a credit or debit card for an items or services exert cautious and be mindful of others. Do not verbally relate any pin numbers or personal information at time of payment.

• During ground travel to prevent possible sickness dine in chain restaurants with established cleanliness policies. In all restaurants always check for cleanliness in the bathrooms prior to ordering a meal. If the bathroom is dirty and this is what the customer sees, is the kitchen clean? Never eat unpackaged counter foods and always check the expiration date on any shelf item.

• Continuance of medical dietary wellness may require specialized foods to be carried on the trip. It is essential at the destination that the host meal preparer be made aware of any and all special diet nutritional needs or allergies.

Air travel reminder and regulation list:

• Make arrangements at time of purchase of airline ticket for senior assistance for transport to departure gate and from arrival gate if needed.

• Allow for additional time when arriving at the airport beyond what is recommended by the airline for engagement of senior assistance and/or the additional time for passage through required processing procedures and to reach departure gate at a personal pace.

• Prior to time of departure make sure scheduled pick-up will be available upon arrival and have the ability to notify if a flight delay is occurring.

• Liquid medications containers of over 3.4 ounces, some medical devices and special toiletries will need to be placed into checked baggage. Contact the ticketed airline for their policies as to what medical devices can be carrier on board the airplane for use during the flight to include portable oxygen concentrators and ability to directly plug in for use, to recharge batteries or use flight supplied oxygen as needed.

• Do not put necessary daily medications into checked baggage because of the possibility of baggage loss. Always carry the days required medications and inhalers needed on one's person with all other medications and immediate need items in the carry-on baggage.

• Traveling with medications within the TSA (Transportation Security Administration) rule and regulations.

o It is not required to notify the TSA security checkpoint agent of any medications or for the medical reason that are being carried on one's person or in a carry-on bag unless liquids. Medications and supplements can be carried in their individual labeled containers or pharmacy vials with prescription information, independently in a pill box or both. There is no limitation on amount or medications carried for personal use.

o The TSA 3-1-1 liquid carry on rule: Individual pourable liquids or gels of sampling size or contained in sealable bottles of 3.4 ounces (100ml) or less placed into a quart size zip lock or a see-through plastic pouch can be transported in carry-on baggage. TSA approved liquid transport kits can be purchased at most pharmacies or online.

o   Nitroglycerin tablets and sprays for heart disease are permitted.

o   Inhalers, hypodermic syringes, diabetic testing devices and supplies, vitamin tablets and other over the counter tablet drugs are permitted.

o   Jet lag effects and time change adjustments of medication intake should be discussed with primary care physician prior to travel.

•   Metal implants within the body will sound an alarm when passing through the metal detector and alerts TSA security officer of the necessity for additional scrutiny. The passenger will be asked to step aside for a physical pat down from an agent of the same gender and possibly a handheld scanning wand will be employed as part of the search process until the TSA officer is satisfied of the authenticity of the medical implant. TSA will not accept for proof of a medical implant a letter from a physician or X-ray as confirmation. Exterior worn therapeutic braces with metal will obviously set off the alarm and require scrutiny with visual confirmation being all that is normally required if brace is easily observable.

•   Laptops are inspected by being passed through the X-ray tunnel at TSA checkpoint in a bin or on the belt. Laptops exceeding 12" x 14" or larger must be removed from bag prior to scanning and processed alone without power cords, cables, optional disc and other accessories in a TSA supplied bin. Remove net books and tablets from carry-on bag and place on belt for scanning. To save time of removing laptop from carry bag one can use an approved laptop carry bag that is TSA friendly. It is recommended that because of the possibility of changes to regulations concerning carry on or checked electronics that the passenger check with ticketed airline or the TSA Contact Center for latest regulations and rules.

• Electronic E-cigarettes, vaporizers, vape pens, atomizers and nicotine delivery devices are prohibited in checked baggage but can be carried on one's person when passing through the TSA checkpoint. The airlines require that prior to entering the cabin all such devices be stowed in carry-on luggage. They cannot be used during the flight.

• Wear comfortable and responsible clothing without metal buttons, clips or hooks and shoes that are easily removed and slipped back into.

• Carry on gifts should not be wrapped to allow for ease of inspection. Place wrapping paper with gift for later use.

• For additional detailed information go online to TSA Travel Tips – Traveling with Medications. Passengers with disabilities can call the TSA Cares help line 1-855-787-2227 weekdays 8 am to 11pm or weekends and holidays 9 am to 8pm EST for answers to questions and advice. Deaf or hard of hearing can use a relay services or be assisted by another during the call.

RETIREMENT EMPLOYMENT

Motivation for retirement employment for healthy and active independent senior citizens varies with each individual from financial necessity, social interaction and a release from boredom. After retirement employment can also be a personal must for an active senior and a way to put to use the skills learned over the years.

Experience, physical ability and senior's decision of the number of working hours per week obviously will play an important role in acquiring retirement employment. Career field employment is not always available in a reasonable senior's travel area that also matches the preferred hourly schedule and presumed value of services to be rendered. An employer of seniors is normally only interested in augmenting staff as needed with experienced part time employees. Normal employment opening is for office functions, store customer assistance, unfilled schedule time slots, seasonal overload, as a helper in the trades with moderate physical labor or with the abilities to assist others with disabilities

If a decision, for whatever reason, is made to include employment activities certain considerations should be evaluated.

- Whether to change direction into a new field of endeavor or stay within the employment experiences of pre-retirement positions.

- Pre-establishment what type of employment desired or what will be acceptable based on job openings in proximity of the seniors' home.

- Available part time employment opportunities can be found in the local newspaper, local job listings sites and internet by entering: Part Time Employment for seniors with city and state added. This will bring up information on current opening. The list will constantly change as openings are filled and new openings are listed.

- Prepare a short résumé with past employment, skills, education and references from former employers concerning ability to perform tasks and on time reliability if applying for a professional position. For base employment positions the filling out of the workplace application will be sufficient. Attachment of a résumé to the workplace application could be a benefit in the selection process.

- A decision of an approximate length of time a retired senior will want to be employed should be part of the equation when deciding full or part time employment. A trained full-time employee is difficult to replace, and this is why almost all senior employment is part time fill in positions.
- Availability of reliable transportation to and from employment.
- Number of hours, days, time of day of employment and employer dictated flexible schedules can impact the seniors overall planned retirement activities.
- Hourly rate, benefits if applicable but very unlikely, flexibility of hours in an emergency.

There is no effect on Social Security retirement benefits on amount of income earned if the senior is of full retirement age. Federal and State income taxes will still apply. If retiring early at age an excess earned threshold figure applies and any amount earned over the threshold will affect social security income. For every $ 2.00 earned $ 1.00 will be deducted from the benefit. The excess earned threshold changes yearly and should be discussed with an accountant or research on the internet by entering: Social Security Income limits after retirement. If earnings are under the threshold there is no penalty.

Home based part time or full-time employment for active seniors and those with limited mobility is away to earn additional income and a feeling of self-accomplishment. Depending on one's professional background and learned abilities there is a wide range of possibilities for home employment or small business startup. Home employment opportunities can be bookkeeping, tax preparing, customer service representative, tutoring, translating and a large variety of computer related positions to include simple data entry to name a few. Home small businesses opportunities are bolstered with the ability to market products on the internet though establish e-commerce sites. Craft based produced products using learned skills in such fields as jewelry design and making, clothing accessories, knitting, embroidery, quilting, ceramics, classic toy making, ethnic Christmas decorations, candles, soap, art of all types and specialty products made from family secret processes. Franchises with established products and markets that can be operated and managed from home are available, but an initial investment is required.

Test market any product initially online prior to full evolvement of effort and monies. Establish a business and marketing strategy plan based on the number of hours per week to be inversed into the project once it is determined to be a viable product.

Be wary of self-employment scams that require a purchase of materials and a promise of marketing the finish product. Research each possibility prior to any investment or involvement.

Volunteering at a nonprofit organization is personally rewarding and away to be socially active meeting new friends with the same civic service principles. There are many locally based nonprofit organizations with varying objectives that are always in need of well-meaning assistance. A senior can select the cause that will be most personally rewarding and become part of the effort to make life better for others.

The need for volunteers at nonprofit organization will differ based on their targeted objective and outreach programs. A senior citizen volunteer can participate by offering to be of service in whatever capacity needed to accomplish the organizations goals. Services offered can be driving older seniors to medical appointments, church or senior activities, delivery of meals and shopping for groceries for the home bound, be a companion and confidant, assistance within house programs and fund raising to name a few. Call the nonprofit of personal choice and ask what assistance is needed and relate personal background information, experience and skills that would be of benefit.

Volunteering for a political party during election cycles is also worthwhile and is away to meet and converse with individuals with the same view.

Most individuals through the years have thought of and dreamed of what they would like to do if only they had the time. As a retired senior now is the time to fulfill that dream.

LAST WILL & TESTAMENT AND FINAL ARRANGEMENTS

Everyone should have a last will and testament no matter the adult age. A will can be drawn up to ones wishes by an attorney or there are online standard forms that can be used to convey wishes for estate distribution. If an online form is used be sure to have it dated and notarized. Two copies should be available. One copy with the attorney who drew up the will or in the use of a on line format be sealed and given to a trusted relative who has also been specified on the last will and testament as the executor receiving a predetermined percentage for executing the provisions of the will. A copy should be sealed in an envelope and filed with other important papers in the home. It is recommended that to prevent a long expensive will probate battle over who gets what two steps can be made. The first is to write in detail in the will or on a notarized list of which household items, jewelry, family heirlooms etc. are bequeath to whom. The seconded which the attorneys do not like, it stops litigation, is to make it clear in the will that anyone initially named should contest the will, for what every reason, be removed from the will with zero entitlements. The removal of the contester/s will prevent any unwarned claims and ensure that the terms of the will be honored as intended.

Final burial arrangements should be made clear in a signed written statement to be included with the last will and testament and also available separately with the location known to others for quick accessibility. The signed and witnessed written statement assures that final wishes are followed by those accepting responsibility for the burial rites. Instructions for the funeral rites to include preferred funeral home, type of memorial services i.e. religious and/or fraternal, location of final resting place i.e. cemetery and burial plot, below or above ground or a cremation with final arrangement for the retention or scattering of the ashes. Whether displayed personal items i.e. jewelry etc. are to be returned or to be a permanent part of the interment. One can also prepare information for the obituary, select grave marker and inscription and a statement expressing good wishes to family members and friends as part of the funeral service.

FRUSTRATIONS OF AGING

Independent senior citizens as they continue to age find frustrations brought about by the managing of many new personal lifestyle changes, understanding the aging process and wellness decisions.

Aging from childhood to now has always been in phases with the senior citizen independent lifestyle being just one of the phases of life's journey. It is necessary to adjust, as in the past, to the physical and mental changes that have occurred from childhood thru adolescences thru young adulthood thru maturity and now to the new senior independent lifestyle. The journey has been long, colorful, eventful, fulfilling, thrilling and with happy and sad times. Use the lessons learned in the past to establish an earned independent senior lifestyle that is comfortable and rewarding.

General senior life style frustrations can be created by agonizing over what has or will occur at time of downsizing of living arrangements to include items retained or disposed of, adjustments to income and spending norms, cost of medications depleting resources, difficulty in doing normal daily tasks, overall physical appearance to include wrinkles, reduced mobility and in some cases boredom and loneliness.

Major senior frustrations can come from the inability to assist a spouse or loved one in their time of need and the unfilled void left by the passing of family members and friends. Additional frustrations can come from stressful medical issues and treatments needed on a regular timeline, limited exposure outside of the home, inability to assist in preparations for family occasions as in the past. The frustration brought about by reduced ability to participate in activities such as getaways, vacations, family occasions, shopping or day trips with family and friends and the inability to do normal daily physical activities. Further the realization of life expectancy with current medical conditions and aging can bring about the feelings of frustration due to lack of control over one's own fate. By mentally accepting what is will not change and implementing only self-positive thoughts by not dwelling on what one cannot do but with thoughts of what one can do creating a pathway to adjust negative mental frustrations to positive feelings no matter what the situation.

Restrictions imposed by an ailment/s requiring various specified daily times for medicating to include injections, medications, use of a monitoring device, special private medical care, physical therapy and a specialty diet can seriously curtail daily available time for enjoyable quality lifestyle activities causing a frustrated feeling of confinement. A strict scheduling of a treatment or a series of treatments and possible designated periods of rest spread throughout the day or at inconvenient times can possibly be alleviated with proper time management. With input of the primary care physicians a more time condensed version to include adjustable time periods to allow for a lengthy time slot in each day for an unencumbered time period for personal activities. Thus, reducing the frustration of the lack of personal flexibility that was associated with the stricter originally timetable.

Additional frustrations are caused with more of the actual wellness fulfillment tasks left up to the patient after a medical appointment. The patient is to act as a middleman to accomplish a final resolution causing feelings of resentment of having to do the tasks that should be the responsibility of the medical team. With limited knowledge and not knowing if it is being done correctly a senior has to deal with concurrent issues for a single occurrence. Issues of balancing extended physician appointments with other engagements, medical assembly line referrals and research and/or consultation appointment with the primary care physician concerning additional drugs to offset the side effect of a necessary major medication.

The frustration of dealing with insurance companies, Medicare and pharmacies concerning coverage, cost and availability of prescribed medications can be very overwhelming. Misunderstandings abound with misunderstood medical terms, abbreviations, unpronounceable names of medications and ailments, pharmacy substituted medications either with a generic brand or with same formulation but a different name and pharmaceutical company and incomplete and confusing directions and procedures cause confusion and adds to overall frustration to self-awareness of medical conditions.

As frustrating as it may be that it is necessary in the patient's best interest to request and insist upon an assurance by the issuing physician that the new or changed prescription does not cancel out or reduce the effeteness of a currently medication or the reverse.

A patient must further coronate any problem with the prescription or dosage non-approval by the insurance provider/s at the time of pharmacy pick-up with the physician's office to determine possible change to another approved medication or a generic substitute to include associated cost. Changes to the medication should be subject to the same medication incompatibilities by the physician's office as the initial prescription.

Unless the physician office provides assistance to solve problems with insurance providers the senior will have to contend with the new patient self-administrating medical policies. The senior citizen will need to be self-reliant and handle each problem positively until resolved. Always be aware of one's wellness status and the medications being prescribed effeteness.

The amount of information supplied mostly in technical terms concerning medications, Medicare and insurance providers statements of services rendered, though well intended, just adds to the confusion and frustration for their lack of simplicity. As a senior citizen participation in one's healthcare it is important to scan through the information and do a read of what is important to the patient. This will allow for the evaluation and cost of the care currently being received. Any questions or misinformation should be discussed with the primary care physician at next appointment along with any problems obtaining or the timely receipt of prescription medications which can cause stress and frustration.

End frustration by understand that relief is brought about by accepting the aging process and looking past underlying issues that are out of one's control. Admitting to one's self that life's current phase is now the norm will be the starting point for the shedding of unwarranted frustrations. By channeling one's concept of aging away from the negative aspects to the positive and accepting the senior citizen independent lifestyle phase will help and allow for the enjoyment of the senior years.

Meet each day with optimism and enjoy the earned relaxation time, old and new friends and suitable senior activities for one's age and physical being. Follow the advice and wellness procedures as prescribed by the primary care physician and other medical professionals to maintain current and future health that will allow for a extended senior citizen experience. A large portion of senior frustrations can be alleviated by using common since recommendations put forth in the previous topics.

It is the senior's responsibility to mold the retirement experience to be free of past responsibilities and frustrations by taking positive steps to reach a desired and meaningful new lifestyle.

A self-positive lifestyle can be shared with a spouse or companion and still be centered on one's personal needs, physical wellness and enjoyment of what life has yet to offer. Being self-proactive in one's current independent senior life phase is not being selfish but practical. With a positive attitude a senior is extending life expectance and eliminating the impact of those things that cannot be changed and the feelings of regret of what could have been that frustrates one's life. Further the self-positive lifestyle can be introduced and shared with others to improve attitudes for a better retirement life for all.

Negative thoughts and actions solve nothing.

GROWING OLD IS NOT FOR WIMPS

My background as an entrepreneur for over 35 years prior to the first semi-retirement was running a company that specialized in product devolvement requiring innovative problem solving and production techniques. Working independently or in conjunction with consulting engineers a new product would be developed.

When specialized manufacturing was needed a small subsidiary would be created to do limited production. A few of the products that I have been involved with the development and manufacture over the years are the initial development of the electrophoresis apparatus for DNA evaluation, DNA processing vials, a PAP smear test, drug testing devices, a mobile vehicle satellite tracking antenna for Comsat, patented needle safety device, RFI & EMI shielding of computer housings and many other projects.

After divesting myself from the original company at age 69 I did a 180 degree and opened an authentic antique print art gallery researching and selling original prints from major artist and engravers from the 1600's, 1700's and 1800's at a shop and with a website presents sold prints locally and worldwide. After 8 years it became obvious at my age it was difficult to maintain a ridged schedule, so I closed the art gallery.

With time on my hands and being well aware of the problems seniors must deal with and with the background of problem solving and research a decision was made to write this book in hopes that it will be a helpful guide to understanding the senior citizen years.